D1318615

A65500 369990

Bird Companions

Bird Companions

Lilo Hess

Charles Scribner's Sons · New York

Copyright © 1981 Lilo Hess
Library of Congress Cataloging in Publication Data
Hess, Lilo.   Bird companions.
Includes index.
SUMMARY: Introduces several breeds of birds that
make good pets and discusses how to select, care for,
and breed your bird.
1. Cage-birds—Juvenile literature. [1. Birds as
pets] I. Title.
SF461.H47   636.6′86   80-26787
ISBN 0-684-16874-X

1 3 5 7 9 11 13 15 17 19   QD/C   20 18 16 14 12 10 8 6 4 2

Printed in the United States of America

The pleasure of keeping birds as companions probably started long ago. It is easy to imagine that as far back as prehistoric times when cavemen brought home different birds for food, they might have kept some for their song and their beauty. A long time afterward, when ships began to sail to foreign lands, exotic birds were brought back for profit. At first, only the rich could afford them, but soon they became pets for everyone. In many European villages a cage with a singing bird was hung outside a house or barn, so that the bird could enjoy the fresh air and passersby could be cheered by the bird's song. At weekly street markets many kinds of birds were offered for sale, and people held long debates about the type or species of bird displayed and about the quality of its song.

Today, bird-breeding and bird-importing are done on a very large scale, and many exotic varieties are available to us now that were previously unknown.

It is very important that you select the right kind of bird as your pet. Your bird should do the things you want it to, look the way you like, and have a good disposition. It must also be able to live in the place and with the care you can provide.

On the preceding color pages are a few of today's most popular and commercially available birds. Most of them are easy to keep, require a relatively small amount of space, and are hardy if taken care of properly.

In the first color plate you see the ever-popular Canaries. If you like beautiful song and a gentle, cheery friend, the canary is the right bird for you. If you are patient and gentle, a canary can be trained to sit on your shoulder and to take food from your hand.

Wild canaries were imported about five hundred years ago into Europe from the Canary Islands, northwest of Africa. At that time they

were small, greenish-yellow birds. Now, bred in almost every country of the world, canaries have nearly doubled in size and have colors ranging from bright yellow to white, greenish, buff, orange, red, and even slate gray. Some species have hoods or crests, ruffles or frills.

Male canaries are trained to sing when they are very young, usually by older birds or from recordings of singing birds; the female does not sing. Each variety of canary has its own type of song. The Roller has a beautiful, lyrical song like an opera singer; the Chopper has a loud, cheery, repetitious song; the Warbler's song is of medium volume with great variety; and the American Singer is somewhere in between, with a sweet song of medium volume.

Until the mid-1930s the canary was the undisputed king of the feathered pets. About that time it was upstaged by a colorful, noisy, mischievous extrovert called the Parakeet, or Budgerigar (Budgie, for short), which you can see in the second color plate. This bird belongs to the parrot family and originated in Australia. In the wild the budgie lives

in large flocks, and its color is green with a yellow face and some black markings. Through selective breeding, today's budgies come in all colors of the rainbow. They can learn to imitate human speech or to whistle a song if they are patiently taught. They seem to love to play with little objects and can learn simple tricks. Budgies are very affectionate and sociable birds, but they tire easily, and their owners will soon see when their pet wants to play and when it needs to be left alone.

In recent years the Large Parrots as well as the Small Parrots have become popular. But unless you have some experience in keeping birds or have someone to help you with their care, you had better start with a bird that is simpler to keep.

The large parrot in the third color plate (double yellow head) and all the other three hundred and more species live in tropical or semitropical climates. Since primitive times parrots were considered very desirable pets. Parrots are brilliantly colored birds with powerful, hooked beaks that can inflict serious wounds. They are active, noisy, gregarious birds, with temperaments that are not always predictable. They are strong flyers and have stocky, grasping feet. A parrot, just like a person, can be left- or right-handed. Parrots eat a variety of seeds, fruits, and vegetables. They can grow very old; some records show them to live thirty or forty years.

Very few species of large parrots are bred in captivity. The majority of the birds sold in this country are imported from Africa, South or Central America, or Mexico. For every imported parrot offered for sale, many others had to die. The methods of capturing them are usually rough. Most animal collectors chop down the tree in which the parrots have a nest. The babies that tumble out of the nest, if they are not hurt too badly, are taken. If the parents attack the collectors, they are shot.

Most imported parrots are brought into this country illegally. Smuggling parrots is a "good" business, because parrots can be sold for a few hundred dollars or many thousands. The birds are drugged so that they will stay quiet, and then they are stuffed into suitcases or inner tubes for the transport. If people would refuse to buy the illegally imported birds, they could help the wild ones to survive a little better.

Many varieties of the Smaller Parrots breed easily in captivity. The Lovebird in the fourth color plate is one of them. You can distinguish a lovebird from a parakeet when you see them side by side: lovebirds are stocky and have short, rounded tails, while parakeets are slender birds with pointed tail feathers. All are beautiful and entertaining pets, but the budgie and the Cockatiel are easier to keep for a beginning bird fancier.

The lovebirds and the other small parrots originally came from Africa, Madagascar, and South America. They all have reputations for being noisy and aggressive birds. When they are hand-tamed as babies they do become tame and learn to talk. Never keep them in the same cage with other species of birds, though, no matter how gentle they seem toward humans, since they may fight other species fiercely.

The friendly cockatiel in the fifth color plate is an ideal small parrot for the beginning *aviculturist* (a person keeping and breeding birds). It has a very good disposition and can be kept alone or in pairs.

The cockatiel is eleven to fourteen inches long—about twice the size of a budgie—and has beautiful plumage and a showy crest that can be raised and lowered at will. You can tell the sexes apart after the cockatiel is about six months old. The male has more of the bright yellow coloring on the head and crest than the female. The female's outer tail feathers are barred; the male's are solid gray.

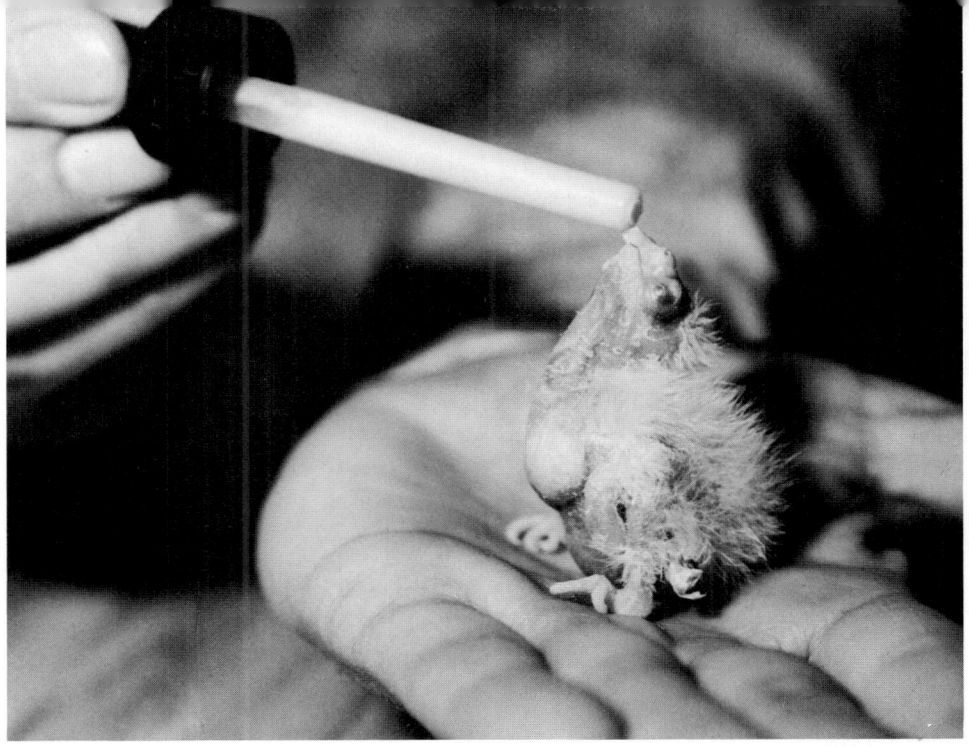

Try to get a bird that was hand-fed when it was young, and it will already be quite tame. Treat your cockatiel gently and never startle it. It learns tricks, imitates human speech, and becomes extremely devoted to its owner. Either male or female makes a good pet, but males are supposed to learn to talk quicker. Females will also learn to talk, but it takes a little more time and patience to teach them. Females, on the other hand, learn tricks faster and are usually more affectionate than males.

If you don't have time to train and play with your feathered pet, but enjoy their beauty and lively antics, get a pair or more of the little exotic Finches, like the ones pictured in the sixth color plate. Most of these delicate birds seldom become really tame, but they will learn to know and trust you and twitter excitedly when you approach. There are about a thousand different species of finches known. They are found in Africa, Australia, and Malaysia, but most that are offered for sale in the United States have been bred in captivity.

Among the many varieties, probably the most popular ones are the zebra finch and the Java ricebird, or Java sparrow, as it is sometimes called. The latter originated in Java and Bali. It sometimes quarrels with smaller finches, but it is one of the few finches that can become quite tame and can be taught to sit on your finger and take bits of food from your hand or lips.

The zebra finch, originally from Australia, is probably unexcelled in popularity among finches, because it can be tamed and is hardy and lively. Also, it breeds so easily in captivity that hardly any are imported anymore. The male has bright red-brown cheek patches and black-and-white, zebralike stripes on its throat and chest. The female lacks the bright colors.

14

One of the most colorful birds in the world is probably the little Gouldian finch from Australia. It has all the colors of the rainbow on its body. It is not easily kept or bred in captivity, however. This little bird is extremely sensitive to temperature changes, which means that it should not be kept in a home that has cooler temperatures at night than during the daytime.

A rare finch that is sometimes found in a pet shop is the whydah from South Africa. During the mating and breeding season the male grows an extremely long tail, which he loses as soon as the season is over.

Plate 1. (left to right) Top: Border Canary, Crested Canary
Bottom: Variegated Buff and Green Canary, White Canary, Frilled Canary

Plate 2.

Parakeets,
or Budgies

Plate 3.   Parrot

Plate 4.   Lovebird

Plate 5.   Cockatiel

Plate 6.   Finches
(left to right) Top Row: Gouldian, Zebra, Silverbill, Hodgson's Rose Finch,
Shafttail, Cuban Melodious, Black-hooded Nun
Middle Row: Cherry Finch, Cutthroat, Red-eared Waxbill, Pectoral
Bottom Row: Olive Cuban, Waxbill

For a different kind of pet, some of the fancy Pigeons, small Doves, and the tiny Japanese or button Quail are interesting and easy to keep. The little quails are probably the most popular ones, with ringneck and diamond doves close behind. The quail is related to the pheasants and can be fed on a diet similar to young poultry. They like to scratch and take dust baths in the sand.

All the birds we have mentioned so far are *seed eaters*, even if they eat some fruit or vegetables to supplement their diet. Seed-eating birds are usually easier to keep than *soft-bills*, which are birds that live on insects, fruit, meat, and eggs.

One soft-bill that is not hard to keep is the Mynah, a bird related to the Starling. Most mynahs we see here for sale are birds that originated in India or Africa. (There are several other species of mynah that are not as common.) Mynahs are probably the best talkers in the bird world, and their vocabulary can be very large. Their words are often so appropriate that it is hard to believe they do not know their meanings. A mynah can only be tamed and learn to talk well when it is young. Mynahs need a roomy cage and a great variety of foods. Fruits, rice, dogfood, hard-boiled eggs, meats, and cereals are just some of the things they eat and should have regularly.

Once you have decided what kind of bird you would like to have, you must think of where to buy it. A good independent breeder is usually much better than a pet store, but a clean pet store is better than a breeder who overcrowds his birds and does not keep them clean. Let's go on a make-believe shopping tour to see what you should look for in a bird and in some of the equipment you need to keep your pet happy and healthy.

Regardless of the kind of bird you are looking for, only select one that is bright-eyed, active, and has tight, slick plumage. It should not have scaly legs or long, crooked toenails. The top part of its beak should not protrude excessively over the lower part. Although the beak and the toenails can be trimmed, excessive length shows that the bird has had very little care.

Don't buy a bird that is listless or has feathers that are puffed up, which usually means it is not feeling well. If you see a lot of feathers on the bottom of the cage or clinging to the wire and perches, the bird might be in molt. The molt is the shedding and regrowing of feathers that all birds go through once a year. At this time the bird can be sluggish and have little interest in food. Canaries, for instance, usually don't sing during this period. Special molting foods are available and should be fed to a bird during this period to stimulate the appetite and provide extra vitamins and minerals. The molt might last two or three months. In any case, although molting is normal, don't buy a bird in this condition, because it is more susceptible to colds and chills at this time. Reliable breeders will not sell their birds until all the feathers have grown back.

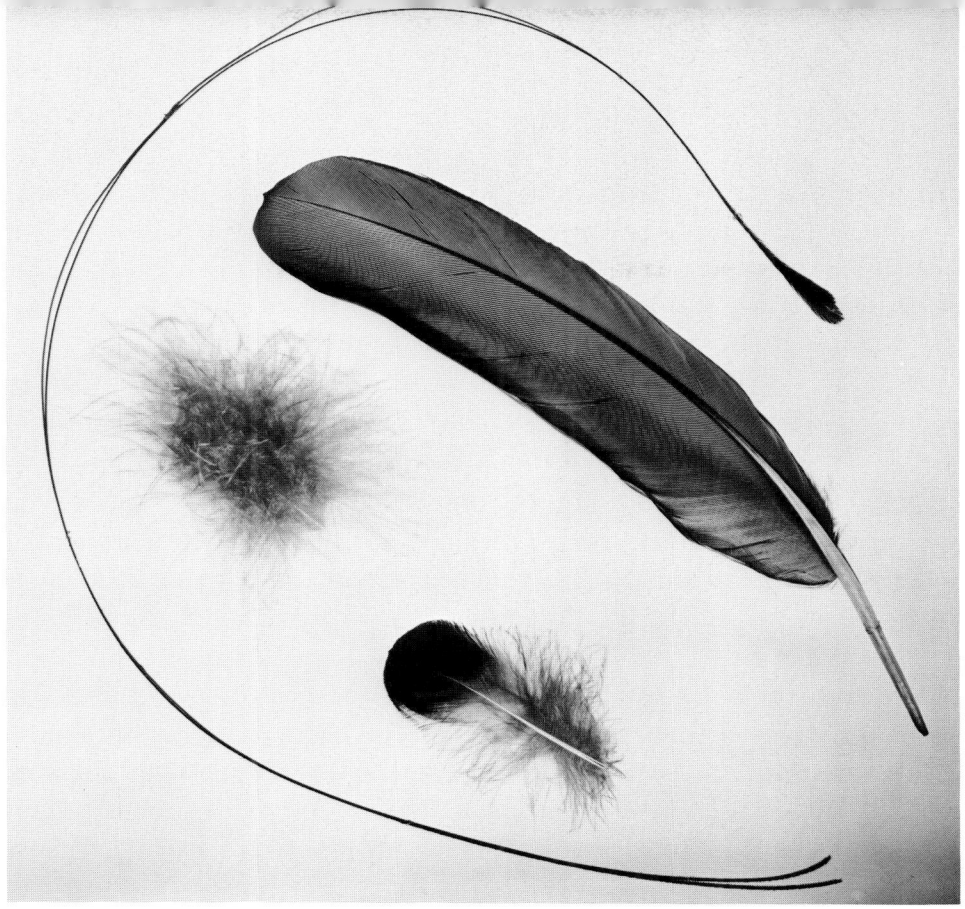

A bird's feathers have several functions. They help the bird to fly, keep it warm in winter and cool in the summer, and they give a bird its shape and its shimmering beauty. Feathers come in a great variety of shapes and sizes, but basically there are only four types of feathers on a bird: the long, stiff flight feathers on the tail and on the wings; the contour feathers, which shape the bird; the soft, downy feathers that insulate the bird against varying temperatures; and the strange, hairlike *filoplume*, which is found scattered throughout the regular feathers. The filoplume's function is not fully understood. In some birds the filoplumes are long and decorative; in others, like our cage birds, they are short, thin, and barely visible.

After you have selected an active, healthy bird, you must look for a suitable home for it—a cage. Just as we humans would not like to live in cramped, uncomfortable surroundings, your pet must have a clean, cheerful, and roomy cage. It is cruel to put a bird into too small a cage, just because the cage is available or fits the decor of the room.

Canaries like to fly and hop from side to side, so their cage should be fairly long and the perches arranged so that the birds can spread their wings. Cockatiels, budgies, and the other small parrots like to climb up and down, as well as fly from perch to perch, so their cage must have height as well as length. Large parrots need a good-sized cage and also an open stand on which they can perch, climb, and stretch their large wings. Some ground birds, like the little quails, need a cage that is long enough so that they can run about on the bottom. Doves and pigeons like to perch high, as well as walk on the ground.

Although the little finches are so small, their cage should be fairly large, since they fly more than they hop. The wires of their cage should be close together so that they cannot squeeze through. They seem to prefer a cage that has a solid back and sides, with wire just on the front and top. Parrot-type birds need all-metal cages, since they might chew up a wooden one.

The perches in the cage should not all be of the same thickness, and they should not all be round. Get some natural branches or twigs, preferably of the fruit wood variety—they are good for a bird's leg muscles, and look very decorative, besides.

Get a birdbath to hang on the door of the cage. A dish on the bottom of the cage—heavy enough so that the birds can't tip it over and large enough for them to get into—is also fine. Let the birds bathe a few times a week. If your bird does not like to use the bath, get a plant mister and spray the bird with room-temperature water from time to time. That will encourage it to preen—clean its feathers.

Before you are ready to take your pet and its cage home, you must still get food, food dishes, and gravel.

Each species of bird needs different seeds and supplements. The

breeder or store clerk will tell you what is good for your bird, and manufacturers' labels also specify for which bird the food is intended, what it contains, how much to feed, and how often. Be sure to buy cuttlebone for calcium and "treats" or "treat-cups" for vitamins and minerals. In addition, you can give your pet some greens, such as spinach (lettuce often is too laxative), chickweed, and celery tops. Grated carrot, a slice of apple or orange, and even a bit of banana is enjoyed by most birds a few times a week.

Your bird's food dish should always have some seeds in it. Birds eat very often. Sometimes a dish might look full, but if you check closely you might find only empty hulls left. If you blow on the dish the hulls will fly off and the full seeds will remain.

The canary's food dish should be hooded and hang on the side of the cage. Budgies and other parrots prefer to feed out of open dishes that are on the bottom of the cage. All birds must have fresh water at all times.

The gravel is usually spread on the bottom of the cage, but it can also be placed in a separate dish. All seed-eating birds need gravel to help grind up the food inside their stomachs.

If your bird has tiny spots on its skin, they might be parasites. Get some dusting powder and sprinkle it between your pet's feathers immediately.

The spot in the house you select for your bird to live should be free of drafts and not in direct sunlight; yet, it must be bright and cheerful. Leave your bird alone for the first few days, except for routine care, of course. Don't try to teach it tricks or expect it to sing until it has adjusted to its new home. Be patient and don't make loud noises or sudden quick movements if the bird is very shy. It only takes a few days for most birds to relax and know your voice and ways.

One of the most interesting and enjoyable parts of bird-keeping is watching baby birds hatching, being fed, and growing up. But before you start a breeding program, think about what you will do with the babies you'll have. Can you keep them all? Do you know someone who really wants them? People often say they would like a bird, but when the time comes to take it, they find that it is not possible after all. Do not breed more than you can handle. It is easier to remove an egg from the nest right after it is laid and not let it hatch than to let a young bird suffer neglect because it is not wanted.

For breeding, make sure that the parent birds are young and healthy and that you have a pair. Male and female canaries look alike, but only the male sings; the hen just twitters. Budgies are easy to tell apart: on top of their beak is a fleshy part called *cere*. In males the cere is blue, in females brown. If the forehead of your budgie is striped, it is an immature bird and too young to breed; adults have no stripes. Male cockatiels have a bright yellow head, which the females lack. Doves and pigeons usually pair themselves off—otherwise you'd do better to consult an expert, since the difference between males and females is very hard to tell. Male finches are much more brightly colored than the females.

The best time to breed canaries is from November through June. About one month before you want to breed them, start feeding them small amounts (half a teaspoon) of soft foods in addition to their regular diet. The soft food can be either the commercially prepared mixture sold as nesting food, or conditioning food, or you can make your own by mixing grated carrot, finely chopped hard-boiled egg, and moistened bird biscuit.

Separate the male and the female canaries with the removable wire partition that is standard equipment if you buy a breeding cage. In a homemade cage, use ½-by-1-inch wire and fasten or tie it so that it can be easily removed.

After a few days the male will sing loudly and strut up and down in front of the female. When you see the male feeding the hen through the wire, it is time to remove the partition. Give them a nest shell and some nesting fibers, both of which you can buy at a pet store. Feed them a little greens and double the amount of the nesting food.

After the canaries have built their nest, the female will lay her first egg. Most breeders remove each egg as soon as it is laid and substitute an artificial egg, which can be bought at a pet store, for each removed egg. Store the real eggs carefully and, after the last egg has been laid, return all of them to the nest and remove the artificial ones. The reason for all this is that baby canaries have a better chance to survive if they all hatch at the same time; otherwise the first hatched baby is about a week older and much stronger than the last hatched baby. Two to six eggs are the usual number a female will lay. Her nest of eggs is called a clutch.

The baby canaries hatch after fourteen days of incubation. They are pink, blind, and have a covering of down. Both parents feed them, but you must provide the parents with plenty of fresh food. Give them the same kinds of food you have been giving them during the nesting period, but in larger amounts. Do not put in all the food at once; instead, feed them three times a day, and remove all the uneaten food.

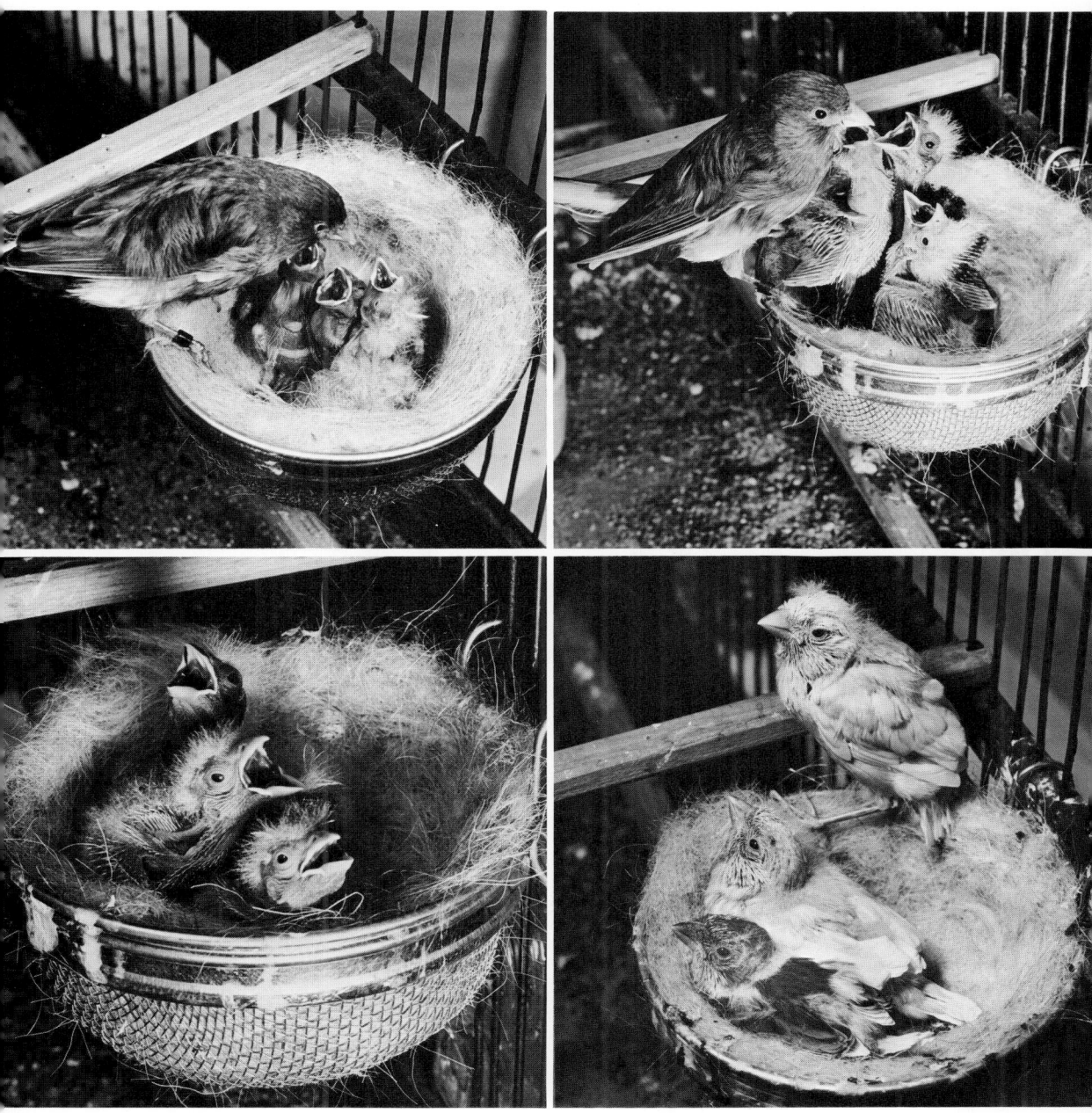

The young canaries open their eyes on the tenth to the twelfth day. New feathers called pinfeathers sprout after the tenth day, and a week later the babies are fairly well-clothed in regular feathers. On the nineteenth day usually one or the other of the babies ventures to the rim of the nest, and in a few more days all the youngsters are hopping in and out. They leave the nest permanently on about the twenty-second day.

There are two different kinds of baby birds: the *precocial* (pree-ko-shul), which means "early ripe," and the *altricial* (al-trish-ul), meaning "nursing." The early-ripe babies are the ones that can run and search for food as soon as they have hatched, like the little chicks and all poultry and game birds. The nursing babies are helpless and need their parents to look after them for a while. All our songbirds and cage birds, as well as owls and other birds of prey, belong to this group.

If you want to breed your parakeets, you do not need to separate the sexes unless you introduce a new bird. In such a case, keep the two birds side by side, each in its own cage or in a divided breeding cage for a few days.

Budgies can be bred all year around and all you have to do is provide a nest box, available in pet stores, and good food. While canaries make an open nest similar to most of our wild birds, birds related to the parrot family need closed boxes with an opening just big enough for the bird to get through. In the wild they use holes in trees.

A week after the nest box has been installed, the female budgie will lay her first egg directly on the wooden floor of the box. Some breeders prefer to line the nest box with cedar shavings—this keeps the box cleaner, prevents the eggs from rolling about when the adult birds hop in and out, and keeps parasites away from the baby birds.

One egg is laid every other day. The average clutch is six eggs. Budgie breeders do not remove the eggs, so the nest contains babies of different ages. It takes eighteen days for the eggs to hatch.

Both parents feed the young with a partly digested mixture regurgitated up from their stomachs called *pigeon milk*. After the babies have been fed, you can see the milky-white substance in their full crops, a pouch-like enlargement of the throat. The babies leave the nest when they are about four weeks old. At that time they should be put into a cage of their own.

29

Pigeons and doves construct a sloppy nest on a shelf or in a corner of the cage, or you can provide a shallow bowl. Give them a few twigs or straw or even pine needles, and the hen will soon lay her two whitish eggs. The hen incubates the eggs during the night; the cock takes his turn till about four in the afternoon, and then the female returns and takes over again. The babies hatch on the seventeenth or eighteenth day. Both parents feed them on pigeon milk, and the young leave the nest after about five weeks. At that time the young are as big as their parents.

Birds are small and fragile in stature, but they are giants in bringing companionship, affection, and fun, as well as music and a splash of color into our lives. Observing and caring for a pet bird gives us insight into the life of a creature very different from ourselves, yet complete and perfect in its own way.

INDEX